Love's Many Names

LOVE'S MANY NAMES

Poems by

Sam Davidson

❦

Introduction and Notes by
Luke Bell, O.S.B.

✠ Angelico Press

First published in the USA
by Angelico Press
© Sam Davidson 2018

For information, address:
Angelico Press
169 Monitor St.
Brooklyn, NY 11222
www.angelicopress.com

pbk: 978-1-62138-392-5
cloth: 978-1-62138-393-2

Cover image: Joel Whybrew and Starra Clarke
Cover design: Michael Schrauzer

To Sylvia Joan Holl

CONTENTS

PART II: KURDISH SONGS

PART III: TWENTY-FIRST CENTURY KARMA

INTRODUCTION

THESE poems have an extraordinary depth and range. The freshness of primordial feeling flows through them, as water drawn from a well so deep that it reaches down to the beginning of time, when all was new and all was possible. Reading them, one feels that one is witnessing the recovery of primeval nature, straight from the hands of God, wild and beautiful. The poetic process is caught in "Adam and Eve It," whose title refers to the first age and (in Cockney rhyming slang in which it means "believe it") to that faith which establishes contact with God who renews it. Shifting syntax unfolds the developing meaning: "The world is"—newly created; "The world is wearing"—growing old, tiring people; "The world is wearing words"—the world is perceived through language, which clothes it; "The world is wearing words out of need"—because words are necessary for its apprehension; "need / To shout itself"—to make itself known; "To shout itself awake in you"—God's spirit speaks to the poet of his calling to allow the world to awaken itself in him and his writing.

It is an awakening like the resurrection of Christ: "Light pours into this volcanic cave . . . where we have come to learn the name of love," as the poet puts it in his reflection on Saint Mary Magdalene, who brought the news of the resurrection to the apostles of the Lord of love. Learning "the name of love" is the whole burden of this collection of poems. The search for it leads to mystery, to the "nameless nothing lurking in our love." We can say to the Lord of Love, "It was for love that you came here... For love you took the name of shame"—but can we say the word that sent the Word? We cannot presume to be definitive, for "Love had many names before we came / To pin her to our lapels like a red flag."

Yet poetry is something other than definition: it is an opening to what is beyond definition, a receptivity to the infinite. This poetry takes us into the presence of "silence breathing in and out," the creative Spirit at work, so that its inspiration becomes ours and "it fills us with His presence for today." In its looking back towards "the primal spark" when the Spirit moved upon the face of the waters, it echoes her "many names before we came" so that listening to what says and does not say her, we may, on the cusp where miracle meets impossibility, hear her.

Speaking "many names," these poems are articulated in the language of multiple traditions. The poet can say, "I will be a Jew" and have laid upon his tongue "words in which Christ's lullabies were sung." He can say to the Madonna, "I was with Jesus on my own / High up that hill, mother, far away" and beg her "take me back." With the Sufi poet Rumi he can say, "There is one alone and only one" and "breathe in / The one and hundred names." His poems reach to wherever "the eternal soul of man" has been touched by the "Shekhinah," the "Sacred feminine," the "Queen of Night." They reach to "churchbells from before churches" so that they become (to borrow another poet's words) "Churchbells beyond the stars heard, the soul's blood / The land of spices, something understood." They reach towards that to which sacred traditions point: the beauty of the one "eternal song."

This collection is divided into three sections. The title of each relates to an aspect of love. The first, "Songs About Nothing," concerns what Iris Murdoch has called "the blank face of love," or, in theological parlance, the apophatic: speaking of the mystery of the God who is love by denying that any positive statement can present Him. Looking in this fashion, the poet says, "I see / Nothing in this emptiness." His art is to evoke that "emptiness" where there is a memory of a "faint, shimmer of breath," to highlight the gap, the "pure tactile darkness" of "silence breathing in and out" so that the reader or listener can, intuitively, be touched by what is beyond the senses. So, for example, he writes in "Falling Leaves":

I was so confused, my mind so full
of light, I tried to hold it, make use of it
it laughed at me, giggling through me, leaves
flashed in front of my eyes, golden, I grasped
but couldn't take hold of them

It is precisely the experience of not being able to grasp the light
that indicates, indirectly, that it is there. To be "full / of light" is to
be "confused." We cannot manipulate love, we cannot take hold
of God, but love can overwhelm us and God can hold us. The
poet's whole art is not a mastery but a being mastered. He cannot
delineate the divine, but his lines can express an experience of
being made relative to—being "laughed at"—by the divine abso-
lute. To enter his poetry fully is to hear "the formless laughing in
the form." He gives us the form, which necessarily can be no
more than a structure of receptivity. The "formless" laughs at it,
for it is a laughable representation of the divine, but also laughs in
it since there we are receptive, and that laughter is the laughter of
light or (to cite another poem) of "the God of laughter, love, and
liberty." It is in the absence of the directing ego that the divine is
present: it is when the poet's "voice drowns into silence" that it
"breathes again / And lives at last upon somebody's lips"—lips
that are "somebody's" rather than the ego's. And so the poet
shows us "this thing / About the absent God, which I cannot
explain"—which cannot be explained by "I" because egoism
blocks receptivity to God. When egotism gives way to receptiv-
ity, when "I" becomes "eye," there is enlightenment, for that is
love.

There is a particular focus for the love and receptivity of the
poet that is reflected in the title of the second section: "Kurdish
Songs." The Kurds are for him as it were a new Israel: close to the
divine source of all, and suffering. Much of this poetry is born of
his direct engagement with them, a compassionate sympathy with
their tribulations as refugees. In the section's opening poem, he
recollects hearing a particular Kurdish song in a refugee camp. In

others he gives a vividly raw account of incidents he witnessed during his months there: young men setting off to try to enter England at risk of their lives; the authorities insisting that the Kurdish flag be taken down; the apocalyptic burning down of the entire camp. His telling is direct, as in: "Muscles made by mountains / Sink through mud / As the nomad staggers forward." The tersely unambiguous language contrasts with the myriad puns that convey metaphysical paradox in other poems, yet essentially the second is similar to the first, as the commandment "Thou shalt love thy neighbour as thyself" is "like unto" the commandment "Thou shalt love the Lord thy God with all thy heart, and with all thy soul, and with all thy mind." Indeed, as a poem in the final section puts it, "everything is love."

"Twenty-first Century Karma" is the title of this section and it points to the spiritual burden of our time: the difficulty of love in the history that falls upon us. "The dead men go to war" and "we continue / Acting out the past." We seem "on course for witnessing the end / Of all things" and yet, if "everything is love," if Saint Paul was right in claiming "all things work together for good to them that love God," if Etty Hillesum was seeing the truth when she found life beautiful and meaningful still as she and her people faced death at the hands of the Nazis, then even "on European streets gloomy with age" there can be hope and happiness. The poet testifies to this:

> I wanted to be happy and I was
> On the edge of all things, tasting dawn
> And drinking night, and thanking love
> For all it has endowed me with

The night, the cup he must drink, does not stop him "from striving to / distil this dawn to pour its light on you" or make him fail to "continue to believe / In creativity." Indeed, creation itself is a miracle of love bringing something out of nothing; it flows from, as the final lines of this collection conclude:

An emptiness that gave birth to itself,
And created, life from a first green seed,
Sap and spit and blood and all the rest of it

Creation, as expressing the Love which is its source, is the poet's theme. For these poems, all of them, are love poems, celebrating *"l'amor che move il sole e l'altre stelle."* Even "many names" cannot capture this love: all they can do is gesture to the silence in which it dwells. It is for the reader to perceive in it "A word of love, like a rhythm /Played steadily on a guitar."

These are poems to be listened to in the heart. They have a richness and subtlety that emerges from repeated engagement with them. You may well prefer to abandon the introduction at this point and begin this and if you do I am happy for you. However, in case it helps to open up the poems for you, I will now give a more detailed exposition of a small sample of them. This is by way of showing how the poetry works, but it cannot confine it to what can be said about it: by definition poetry of this kind is beyond definition, opening as it does to the ineffable. I make no claim therefore to a definite reading: there will be other readings and they will be good. The same is true of the notes at the end of the book. They aim to open a way into the poems and not, God forbid, to pin them down. The poems will always say more than can ever be said about them and in any case an element of the joy in reading them is finding the multiple meanings there. For that reason, the endnotes deliberately make no attempt to be exhaustive even of this one reader's understanding: rather they are designed to encourage and equip you in your entry into the mystery of this poetry.

The first poem to be considered takes its title from a small village, ten kilometres from Dunkirk in northern France: Herzeele. It is here that the poet stayed during the months of his encounter with refugees. The main themes of the poem are announced in the first stanza:

> I dreamed I was washed in the sea
> A body without a boat
> I woke to sun on the farm
> Light-hearted, newly born

This articulates the same spiritual reality that baptism enacts, which is not to say that it is simply about baptism: rather it opens up for us what baptism expresses. The sea is a symbol of eternity and washing in the sea is being made clean and whole by an encounter with the eternal which is undivided. This brings joy (light-heartedness) and new God-given life redolent of these words from chapter three of Saint John's gospel: "Except a man be born again, he cannot see the kingdom of God." It is an awakening to the sun, suggestive of both the resurrection and the love characteristic of this new life. "The farm" is the place where the poet is living and he becomes through his loving identity with the refugees "a body without a boat," for they are stuck in the refugee camp, longing to cross the Channel to England without the means to do so. They have no Moses to lead them across the Red Sea to their promised land. Their situation, and his, is at the heart of the spiritual rebirth that his dream speaks of, just as the second and third lines of the stanza which express this situation are contained within the first and fourth lines which tell of the rebirth.

The poet's situation is established by the following stanza:

> Lazy, I walked in the fields
> Loved, a sad, lost bird
> On artificial hills
> Spring spread her seeds over slag

He walks in the sprout and hop fields that surround the village and is "loved." That is the meaning indicated by the comma following this last word, but with a shifting syntax characteristic of his writing the poet develops its meaning by what follows: he loves "a sad, lost bird." The bird, again characteristically, points to the Holy Spirit, the Paraclete who manifested in the form a dove. Here she is "sad, lost" because the spirit of love is so diminished in our time, particularly in the exclusion of refugees fleeing for their lives. The phrase "a sad, lost bird" can also designate the poet himself: sad and lost because identified with the sorry condition of the refugees affected by the exclusion of the spirit of love, and identified with that spirit. This ambiguity of identity is also very characteristic of his writing, and points to the oneness of humanity, the transcendence of "I" and "you" and metaphysically to the ultimate identity of the knower and the known. The spirit is undivided, like the seamless garment of Christ crucified woven from above, and includes everybody. The "artificial hills" in Herzeele are a result of borax mining and the seeds of spring on them pick up again the theme of rebirth.

In the next stanza the poet's identity is further expanded to include others:

> Old, I died in the soil
> Bones in red, French fields
> Roots hooked round cold fingers
> Scattered waste abroad

Here those who died in war—particularly the First World War— in French Flanders are remembered. The soil to which the refugees from war have come contains the remains of those whose lives have been wastefully lost in some corner of a foreign field.

> A million combat boots
> Fertilised the land
> Fed the hops for beer
> Purified my poems

So many people died here; their bodies are fertiliser for the hop fields. Sharing their suffering, which lives on in that of the new arrivals, purifies the poet's writing. He undergoes a baptism not only of water but also of fire. In this place of anguish, his poetry becomes deeper, born of costly experience. Relative to most of the other poems in this collection, this one is early and it heralds the increasingly mature voice with which they speak.

The purifying of poems by suffering is ultimately the purifying of vision since language is our apprehension of the world. The purifying of vision is preparation for the ultimate, beatific, vision. This is the metaphysical truth underlying the title of "Slow Maturing Bliss," a poem that enacts this transformation of soul. It is in one sense the most universal poem in the collection since all suffer and all are opened to eternal happiness to the extent that they accept their destiny with love, but it is in another sense the most specific poem since it points to "Jesus the author and finisher of our faith; who for the joy that was set before him endured the cross." Hence the poet speaks in the persona of Him, the Universal Man, when he writes:

> Why should I weep, who never had to lose
> this World, but was the Earth by touching her?

As God, he creates the world by perceiving it—His knowledge, His word is creation—so He need never know a loss that causes tears. Yet because He has embraced and entered creation, a joyful mystery, He can say:

> I tasted all her sweetness and I smiled
> to see she loved me too, and how it thrilled

The enjambment that links this stanza to the next dynamically develops this meaning to reveal the Passion that is the concomitant of the Incarnation and makes apparent the price of love. Being made flesh is "to be consumed by soul, by sense, by self." It is also, in Saint Paul's words, "to be sin for us" and so the Saviour can say:

became the teeth that gnawed the heart of life
and moaned, and died, and Death within me died

This last line points to His passion and death and the resulting death of Death. The light of the resurrection follows:

and in his place was new born deathless light

whose white contained innumerable shades
of colour, the black void giving birth to stars

This is a new creation, which is won in Christ who selflessly loses His life (which becomes hidden so that all may share it, becoming stars—saints—in heaven) and therefore can say:

so I drowned in that abyss, and scattered seeds
that sucked your spring, burst blossom in the dark

The poet understands that love is the source of creation and the renewal of creation in Christ—it is the mystery hidden in the suffering in which we are joined to Christ and prepared for bliss— and so He ends with the grateful assertion:

and everything is love, and always was
thank you for reminding me of that

Wonderfully, the poet is able to show without repeating the banalities of piety that even terrible suffering serves love. Because poems such as this come from the heart of experience and are faithful to the truth that is the source and heart of everything they can speak as well to those to whom the conventions of religion are opaque as to those who profess faith.

Such another poem is "Edible Bugs" whose exposition of creation is a veritable theodicy, wonderfully marrying observation of nature and spiritual truth. The first two lines seem simply to present nature red in tooth and claw:

> Seagulls tap the turf, enticing worms
> To sudden death

The seagulls appear merely predatory. However, as noted above, birds are symbols of the Spirit of God at work in the world. God is omnipotent and yet His love chooses the overcoming of His power. Hence:

> ...the weak must feed the strong
> And strength abandon subtle ways to find
> Complete defeat, though it becomes itself

Its becoming itself (or behaving becomingly) is the realisation of the truth of its nature as loving gentleness.

> It must bow, bend to the brink, and shatter
> Brittle from the white heat of perception

The pure and ardent divine gaze or perception (in God knowing is loving) pushes power to where it shatters

> Becoming an eye to love will make one blind,
> Over-brimmed with mercy, love struck stoned

That is, it becomes itself an eye because it beholds with such a loving gaze (love is in the eye of the beholder) and also an "I" and so personal and able to love. However—as the shift in syntax from the qualification of "becoming an eye" by what precedes it to its qualification by what follows it suggests—that eye in its loving transcends its partiality and so becomes blind (love is blind) no longer seeing with a view to its own advantage and thus merciful, effacing the egoism of its "I", love-struck, struck as with stones, stoned as in drugged.

The seagull is now

A drunkard tapping his foot to your constant beat
As you disarm him of his cruelty, pickpocket

Drunk as with love, it is obedient to the divine rhythm and so not cruel. At this point it becomes apparent that the poem is essentially a prayer addressed to the Lord of Life whose "constant beat" is directing all creation. He is a "pickpocket"—a thief, an attribution made several times in the New Testament. The poet says to him:

Your fingers are in all my conspiracies
Your gradual changes in the muscles of my wings
Make them always stronger for wounds you put in them
The caterpillar no longer fears your beak

The Lord writes straight with crooked lines, using "my conspiracies" as in what Joseph says to his brothers who sold him into slavery: "Ye thought evil against me; but God meant it unto good." So the whole of creation is revealed as being governed by love, which conquers fear. The edible bugs are changing into butterflies as their wings grow stronger; the apparent dissolution of the chrysalis makes it possible to fly away. No earthly power can stop anyone going to heaven; being subject to such rather makes souls stronger for the journey.

The metaphysics of this poem is subtle. One way of thinking about it is to say that all subjects are subsumed in the Subject which is transcendentally identified with the Object so the Knower and the Known are one in the identity of Love: the seagull, the bug, the butterfly—all are orchestrated in a single divinely conducted dance. Not predation but Providence is at work, making us lovelier through our very wounds, after the pattern of Christ's glorious wounds. This Providence acts through even the predatory beak so that this is in effect the beak of the Lord of Life (hence "your" beak). That is what the metaphysics underlying the poem implies. The ending is present in the beginning: the seabird is the Eternal Spirit (the sea is eternity, the bird the Spirit) here momentarily concealed by illusion (gulling, misleading) yet working its great work of love. None of the above is to imply that the poem can be reduced to this: each poem is its own language, but writing what parallels it in other language can help it speak for itself—not that it really needs that help, of course.

Wordsworth observed that every author of any greatness and originality "has had the task of creating the taste by which he is to be enjoyed" and he compared this to the difficulty Hannibal had in getting his elephants over the Alps, for which he had "to shape his own road." It is my hope that this introduction and the notes at the end can help with a bit of road clearing. These poems will superabundantly repay the acquisition of the taste by which they are to be appreciated since they are such as, in Shelley's words, "measure the circumference and sound the depths of human nature with a comprehensive and all-penetrating spirit."

Indeed, they have a prophetic power that cannot be identified with anything in this world for "The wind bloweth where it listeth, and thou hearest the sound thereof, but canst not tell whence it cometh, and whither it goeth." This poet has a universal identity. He is simply open to the Spirit, breathing in and, inspired, breathing out "language fresh with power / for primal poetry." Keats famously said that Shakespeare had "negative capability," meaning that he was "capable of being in uncertainties, mysteries, doubts, without any irritable reaching after fact and reason." So it is with this poetry, which does not tie us to any fixed and established course but, open to mystery, simply channels the flow of what is, born of the Spirit and nourished by prayer.

Cato wrote *rem tene, verba sequentur*—"grasp the thing, the words will follow." This poet has seized it—has seized, or been seized by, the ineffable—and the words have followed.

LUKE BELL O.S.B.
Feast of Christ the King 2017

PART I
Songs about Nothing

Fall

Have we lingered so far from the Tao
That there can be no homewards journey now?
Forgiveness being but a pretty word
With which Eve hid her frailty from the LORD,

I want to know if I was ever saved
Who have known love, have loved, and have been loved
Who have destroyed, corrupted, and betrayed
The angel babe in whose form he was made,

Salvation salves, but only pain is real,
As life broke into death, thus flesh learned how to feel
You held it for a moment, then let drop
That space between the breaths where feelings stop.

But what is lost? The poetry of life
Descending now like Orpheos into Hell

Memorial

For almost a year
A refugee camp stood
On the outskirts of Dunkirk
At its height it numbered
Three thousand residents
The majority were Iraqi Kurds
The majority of these Peshmerga
(Those who face death)
Men and women
Young and old
(Mostly young and mostly men)
They had been fighting Daesh
(Isis)
Until they ran out of bullets
Their salaries hadn't been paid
For six months
The money was stolen
By the Iraqi government
Along with the bullets
Nobody died in this camp
But one young man
Was crushed under the wheels of a truck
On the outskirts of Oxford
(Where I was born)
He had been riding on its axle

Landing

I was thrown down, but into what? I see
Nothing in this emptiness but me,
There was a you, a hot, faint, shimmer of breath
As spoken lies disturbed the silent truth

You moved in this, cold air inside cold air,
Dark strands of hair entwined dark strands of hair,
White moonlight folded over fingers white
As blossom blanched by winter of its light.

The pulse awoke, and in its saccharine streams
My hot blood surged, and in your flying dreams,
Unspoken hungers tempted you, and found
New fertile soil, new vigour in the ground,

And I was dead, but death renewed my soul
I sought for you, to haunt, aye but to heal.

Fog of War

At Halabja
Five thousand of them died
To gas at the hands of "Chemical Ali"
Soon after, the West went to war
To the outrage of infant liberals
Such as myself

Nameless Nothing

A new life, vegetable, wired on sap
Surged like a spating river in your lap
Whilst I who lay here wordless watched your lips
Replace what was hinted by our fingertips,

Tap, tap, and in between the touches this
Nameless thing between man and his bliss
This ancient entropy to which heat returns,
This mudra which each broken body learns

Stretched out like a fading actor and his speech
Concluded by a question out of reach,
Anticipated, missed, unspoken-of,
This nameless nothing lurking in our love

Whispers: "I was once a holy thing:
A crown upon a King was I, Nothing."

Elevation

We hung Saddam from a rope
And replaced him with the Shia government
The Iraqi army left their guns and tanks
At Mosul to be salvaged by IS

Yezidis fled to the crest of Mount Sinjar
NATO dropped them food as the wolves crept in
From Syria the People's Units came
And saved a whole race from desolation

Grail Fish

It lies beside you, in its dying voice
The murmur of a choice which was no choice
That whispered to old Moses in his fire,
That tempered and singed the strings of the Orphic lyre,

Which bubbled in a stream of gibberish
Where Finnegan once caught his fleeting fish
And laid it on the pebbles, grabbed his knife
And took it to the waters for a wife,

Where sunk grail kings and trails of drowning knights
Swift to die for artificial lights,
While troubadours and maniacs who kept in tune
Stalked wolves and sang their lovesongs to the Moon

Whilst then beneath the trees where lovers met
There still was warmth, and there the trap was set

Gender Roles

Kurdish men died in such large numbers
Their women graduated into soldiers
In Syria they declared a revolution
Burned their burkas, while in the West
Feminists made friends with Islamists
Having, as they believed, a common foe

Voice in Wilderness

Return into the void: this sweet embrace
Walks with the wind on the desert on your face
Sings to me of what is lost inside you,
Howls for every tenderness denied you

Who now camps by Troy in this old tent
(As Icarus adorns his sweet lament
And stitches feathers, bright and soft, and states:
Here is a pattern worthy of the fates)?

Another woman, coming from the shore
Anoints his wings and genuflects before
The lawless world, and we go down into
Your endless mystery, Eternal Jew

Our tongues in harmony unite in praise
Of what appears in rays but does not blaze

Economics

The poor who flee the war
Rarely become refugees
They are gunned down or turned back
Long before they reach Europe
Consequently the majority in Dunkirk
Were decidedly bourgeois
The ones who could afford to pay

10,000 euros per head
to Albanian people smugglers

The Invention of Fire

Your ceaseless satisfaction bleeds away
As the night does through the punctures of the day
And tear-like balloons rise up in precipice
Over a lip of the world like half a kiss
And we, on this rock, are living among
The best and the worst of the succulent throng
While I drink the dust, you taste the chai of dawn
Flavoured with all the spices of light, reborn

And question comes as we slip into sound
The name of nothing which we have found
Not secret, subtle, sacred, nor profane
No thing is left, not even doubts remain
To stay with us in vigil in the dark
To light a fire: to strike the primal spark

Magdalene

Light pours into this volcanic cave
through a glancing crack in brightly whitewashed stone
heady rays from the desert heights above
blaze in this emptiness we jointly own
where we have come to learn the name of love
and are therefore at last, at last, alone

You move your hand, caressing limbs that sweat
the fevers out as daydreams pass between
our fingertips, and we at once forget
how long we've longed this sickness to set in
remembering not the words, which separate
the breathing self from the sleeping stranger's skin

I open up a wound, you bind it fast
with tangled leaves and wash me of despair
we laze the morning, letting it roll past
stirred but not obliged by the call to prayer
Magdalene I think that I can taste
salvation in the dust that coats your hair

Donatello

Absent

She has a lot of lavender
And coloured clothes to wear
Out in the street her jasmine grows
Her perfumes fill the air

Her lantern glows, and watered rose
Spills through her charcoaled hair
The sky is clear, and spring is here
But something isn't there

Something isn't there, my love
Something isn't there
The sky is clear, and spring is here
But something isn't there

She has a street of innocents
And all of them come down
To free the idols from their tents
And walk them through the town

Their painted eyes still stare and weep
As sweetly as before
But in the lodge where secrets sleep
Something isn't there

Something isn't there, my love
Something isn't there
The sky is clear, and spring is here
But something isn't there

The ships come in from far away
The harbour folk prepare
To unload the Tyrean treasury
And the spoils of holy war

And the peacock feathers which they wave
And the rubies that they store
Cannot decorate my love
For something isn't there

Something isn't there, my love
Something isn't there
The sky is clear, and spring is here
But something isn't there

Jeremiad

He knew he had married a prophet of doom
When she rolled over in her sleep
And said
Atom bomb

Drag

I will walk into the desert
And dye my raiment white
I'll stalk amongst the libraries
Like some itinerant knight
In search of your holy books
Which I didn't help to write
I'll love you like a fugitive
And it will be alright

And I will be a Jew for you
Because that's what you like
And I will break the veil for you
Where it is the most thick
And I will be alone with you
Until my tongue is tired
And I will be a Jew for you
Like when I was inspired

And I will walk away with you
When the sea is red
Behind us like a hologram
Of all the billions dead
In the making of creation
Which I was not there to see
Which you filled with alien unity
As a present just for me

Jerk Hypnic

When I truly want to find out who you are
Wait, come back, I only know who I am
Or lose ourselves forever in the other
And we separate in case we drown
The reality of thinking about the touch
And the dream of real sensation fades into
And we jump like those who have just failed to sleep
Except when I recall how much I long for you
Tongues learning to taste the taste of taste
Peace exploring an infinite world of peace
We are silence breathing in and out
Depart into pure tactile darkness
The tides of fanatics on either hand
Surge like merging particles at sea
The public parted into war parties
Are nothing but two mouths meeting
Divisions and delusions of the world
Is to kiss you, it's extraordinary
When I'm kissing you all I want

Sun of Man

You can't return by the path you came
On and on, go seek the sun
You'll find the way when day is done
Though memories fail, on, to your home

The one you lost to seek yourself
And sink infinity in flesh
Hear echoes of the ocean's crash
And drown yourselves in the waves of life

Forget what it is to be pure
But learn the worth of purity
Shipwrecked, in good company
Beachcombers, battered on a shore

Find soft-rubbed shells, incline an ear
To sounds of your own soft, singing voice
Reminding you, you had a choice
It was for love that you came here

For love you took the name of shame
For love you raised him to a throne
For love you win a losing game
And live eternally alone

Agamemnon

My face is made of gold
My hands cascading jewels
The seas their fingers hold
My countenance it rules

I seed the land with salt
Grow towns from rubies buried
And seize the bonded world
With a grip of bronze, unhurried

My dreams will march on Troy
And ere this night is past
Will conquer and destroy
And feel myself at last

And when the war is done
And when the dream is through
I'll rise and pluck the sun
Out of the sky to give to you

Doe

You looked at me with almond eyes,
All sweated skin and shiny down,
And held my isolated gaze,
Two bodies frozen by the dawn,

I felt the force that bound us both,
Electric-crackling whiff of storm,
The animal conceit of love,
The wordless meanings of a dream,

You startled and were swiftly gone,
A blaze of amber, burning speed
And left me to myself, alone
As sunlight burst into the glade,

I turned away towards the smoke
And heard the voices of my friends,
And sat with them in gentle talk,
And warmed my dirty, human hands

Blank Page

I speak to you, not as infidels do
Who bury with their words a tortured Lord
But as a scribbler comes to write on you
Suras worthy of the living Word

White page I condescend to blot
With printed marks the tongue can really taste
You hold inside you echoes of my heart
Beneath your surface, nothing goes to waste

My voice drowns into silence, breathes again
And lives at last upon somebody's lips
But not until I dare to push my pen
Across you, and I wonder, if it slips

Will I choke up your throat, or must it sing
Regardless of my clumsy suffering?

Anatolia

She sipped her coffee and I wondered if
It tasted to her so sweet as it did to me
Early morning, when the seabird's laugh
Echoed on both coasts of this divisive sea

Smoke she blew drifted blue and soft
Into my own mouth, so I breathed her poetry
I didn't want you here, she said, and yet
Don't leave me now, come further east with me

Drunk, we rode upon a Turkish jet
Like angels through the Asiatic sky
Settled on the desert, and the night
Enfolded her into its mystery

So she wept in my arms, and then at dawn
She left me, on the road to Kurdistan

Transmigration of Souls

Non interire...

I die and am reborn
I die and am reborn
In this camp beyond
Both dusk and dawn

This night beyond
Both right and wrong
Where pilgrims throng
This migrant song
I die and am reborn

Inside the flesh that's torn
Inside the sappy thorn
In pain and pleasure
Stain and treasure

Hymn of night
And horn of dawn
This clarion
Will carry on
I die and am reborn

Out of mud and water
Out of light and laughter
This the prize
In human eyes

The comfort and the torture
In breathing lips
And fingertips
I touch and turn
I live and learn
I die and am reborn

Objects in Space

…sed transire

There can be no sticking here
No sinking in the soil
We must sweep like tides
Like tides of oil
Across the land
Shimmering, mercurial

Pull down our tents
And we will leave no trace
But ashes on the earth
Like armies moving forth
Through a desert place
We are objects in space

Propelled by alien impetus
From the ancient void
Until we crash
Without a word
Into your flesh
And you at last believe in us

Falling Leaves

I was so confused, my mind so full
of light, I tried to hold it, make use of it
it laughed at me, giggling through me, leaves
flashed in front of my eyes, golden, I grasped
but couldn't take hold of them, Autumn so swift
the mountains tumbled after her, snatching at
their stolen robes, so the seas came up
and wet our feet, my toes were foundations
of Empires that decayed in passing thoughts
and then you were there, and all the time to spend
placing each seed into its proper place
from which to grow the new rainforest
I wanted to tell you, it was for you I tasted
death, mud, cigarettes, hope

Sister Exe

How could I know she lit a fire for me?
But into it I gladly would have gone
Still I was uncertain she could burn
The source is not the fuel of ecstasy

Sibyl, simple woman, living witch
I scratched myself until as pale as she
Until my tongue could utter prophecy
Which she need never stretch her arms to reach

How foolish suffering, how meaningless
How painless is the sweet remembering?
How hollow sobs and softly stammering
Love words to one whose love was blemishless

As she, except she was not ever white
But freckled with stars like the infinite night
Downfalling, the comet soars into the sea
And I sink there to seek you, Eurydice

Eurydice, why did you make me go
So far into the dark for you to fade?
It made a joke of everything we had
A joke or song or myth, I still don't know

She says she never asked for you to come
But laid a place there for you nonetheless
Did you eat their pomegranate seeds, confess,
And spend a whole night with her in the tomb?

What was there for you, poor Orpheos,
Who cannot even bargain with the dead?
Did you think she would follow you instead
Who had already found the fount of souls,

Who had already sipped that nectar sweet
Which is where Styx's stream and Lethe meet
And forward into stranger dawns had stepped
And poetry, and all delusions dropped

So did I burn her making her a poem
Or merely show her how to light the spark?
Was it illusion dancing in the dark?
Or the formless laughing in the form?

Love had many names before we came
To pin her to our lapels like a red flag
Act as though ours was all the rage
Ours the serpent, ours the virgin womb

But all of it was nature's crawling legs
Lit by a thousand points of dew-drop fire
Which the morning drops, all monsters to inspire
As they scuttle to bury their seeded eggs

But she went with me into that dragon's cave
And made me first a saint and then a slave
And rose me up, clad in mercurial scales
To coil at her feet and shimmer in her curls

It was the holly king they burned on high
And buried him under a green barrow
He it was who sucked the summer's marrow
And lost his strength that he might learn to fly

But could have studied lucid dreams and only
Died in fantasy, by dawn reborn
But that sensitive flesh must feel the thorn
If it's to know the holy and unholy

But that it must turn into a God
Remembering somehow it was a man
If to begin and know what it began
If to order and endure the flood

And only then somehow enjoy the play
Staying up all night to kiss the newborn day
And daub dancing horses on a cave wall
Denounce the fantasists, but seek the grail

Turned into a book by Robert Graves
He suffered under chaste female poets
Sisters, muses, symphonies, and sonnets
Looking under, Medusa's locks of loves

Ever spinning Christ on a turning wheel
The ouroborus sucking at his toes
He spasms, choking on contorted prose
That poetry might find out how we feel

Sacred feminine, Sappho's heir
Where spark and brushwood meet a human laugh
Ignites the undergrowth, and sets it off
The all-destructive birth of a future star

Prised out of the night, a fitting word
For one to open up Aladdin's horde
Who trickster-quick was there before he spoke
The one who spun a riddle for a lock

Small, so small, made out of spider webs
You couldn't believe it might ensnare the night
Rewrite its doggerel and get it right
The hymn hymeneal of acid tabs

Scratched into dry dust at an oak's foot
Some dirty rhyme written by a child
Raised by howling wolves in the singing wild
For old Catullus to learn upon his lute

Man imitating nature, imitating woman
Imitating God and making music
Out of grunts and agonies of cosmic
Birth, the breaking of the former human

Snaps a fresh shape out of her tiny course
A river makes a new sea, and new shores
And I stand on her bridge, watch her ripples black
As she trickles on, the laughter of the lake

A little girl, a fool on a king's stage
An actor in history for her innocence
Which made her welcome where tyrants dance
So that she traced her own shape on the age

Of poetry, but only poetry would
Make such strange and simple things so grand
Only saints and perverts understand
Only saints and perverts ever could

Therefore I light a candle in her honour
Not for a prayer that I might ever win her
But that I might sing her hymn, a sinner,
Here on my pin-up altar, O ma donna

Here where I lay down my head you find
Your dark fields fertilised, but by the wind
As you flow on through the surging estuary
From riverine dreams to the other mystery

The Absent God

I am, but know not what it is to be,
I am not you, therefore I look at you,

And hold you in my gaze, you sweet enigma,
And for a moment, empty of myself,
Explore that art that holds you in my eye,
Uninvented, except by the naked void,

Whose silence alone can comment on itself,
Speaking volumes of nothing, all about you,
Unaided, our dreams, scattered through the night,
Will dissipate in darkness to darkness' gain

And I will never have to tell you this thing
About the absent God, which I cannot explain,
You know it already, you who reduce me to colours
And stretch my body out like a spectrum of light

Brothers

I dreamed of my brothers underground
Who sheltered me from the night
When I stoked their fires with a shivering hand
And trembled in their sight
As our shadows crossed the withering land
We searched for the nomad light

We sought that light as we fled from the dirt
The frozen, infertile soil
Drinking tides that swept down from the east
Incendiary rivers of oil
Polluted our blood as we slaked our thirst
And what was left living to spoil?

The ocean was ruddy with fire and with blood
My brothers were driftwood upon it
And I, their reflection, was lost in the mud
As it covered the face of the planet
Hiding for shame in the pits of the dead
Like a bomb hidden under a bonnet

I see them pass by me with grim, frozen faces
Hooded, alone down the concrete causeways
Or walking in pairs through some quaint, English places
Safely at home, but running always
Running, for ever the memory chases
Out of the war and the nameless days

PART II
Kurdish Songs

Ishqt

It seemed like a mountain song
As old as the Kurds were young
When it leapt like a butterfly
From a patient pilgrim's tongue

I think it surprised them too
How masterfully it flew
The promise that feeling is real
Which I leave in this poem to you

I can hear it still vibrate
In the space its wings create
The burning lover's hymn
To the beauty of his fate

Oh, let it settle here
On this soft, white, waiting ear
Or soar above the camp
Like a soul who has learned to steer

I Remember Phoenix

I remember Phoenix on the Dover Ferry
Singing the Wild Rover
My voice reached to but could not catch hers
For hers was lifted above the wind
While mine just rode upon it

But once in the farm at Herzeele
We sang together the Wild Rover
And our voices joined together in telling
The tale of the prodigal son
As though it were true

The wind tossed our hair and clothes
Seabirds screeched
Keeping pace with the ship
Phoenix's eyes were the only fixed points
All the rest was ocean

A Vault in the Desert

A sickly tree rooted
In the grave where we were buried
And separated our bones
As though we had fought
In the same war
For opposing nations

Spartans

I like them best like this, at war with life
As they have been, at home, at war with death
I like their eyes, set green between their brows
Their sturdy feet well poised in filthy boots

I like their smiles, their sad defiant songs
Because of that defiance, and because
There is no reason why they should be here
Who might have died on the slopes of Mount Sinjar

I want to stoke their fires, but they must each
Pass into a winter muffled by mankind
From here they must be saved and each, worn down
In his own way, embrace the same decay

And I meander back into my life
Shieldless from the field of Thermopylae

Yes Tor

Every step takes us further from God
Down the mountain path from the peak of Yes Tor
Through banks of swarming midges and mating mayfly
The river on our right, below the reservoir
And all about us the human silence of the moor

You could be forgiven for thinking this was Kurdistan
The cracked volcanic strata, the burning sun
The country far beneath us civilised and small
About us the lawless highland, from which we fall
Back into that other, promised land

Herzeele

I dreamed I was washed in the sea
A body without a boat
I woke to sun on the farm
Light-hearted, newly born

Lazy, I walked in the fields
Loved, a sad, lost bird
On artificial hills
Spring spread her seeds over slag

Old, I died in the soil
Bones in red, French fields
Roots hooked round cold fingers
Scattered waste abroad

A million combat boots
Fertilised the land
Fed the hops for beer
Purified my poems

Desert Confession

She took me out into the desert
on sufferance, for I had learned
to please her with my mouth
and with my Jewishness,
which is not real like her Jewishness,
but earned, like a hangover.

I made love to her underground,
in an old tomb where,
the Pharisees presumed, the soul
must rot for all eternity with the body
until the day of greater dissolution.

She cried and told me I had saved her,
later on I learned she never loved me,
and I wondered, guiltily, if I knew now
what it was like to be Jesus.

Prodigious Sun

I was with Jesus on my own
High up that hill, mother, far away
He told me that I'd always been alone
And that these words were all I could say

Father, Father, I have forgotten your face
You told me "walk" and I walked all the way
Beyond the boundaries of the northern race
Before the shadows fleeing the birth of day

I lost what you gave me, my protective power
My hands grew ugly as a lizard's skin
I was leprous, weak, and in dry rocks did cower
For the fear that water would reflect my sin
Let me drink, mother, let me drink this lake
I see the sky, I beg you: take me back

Seasong

I wasn't lost 'til I came close to home
Haggard on the draft of that red sea
Perceiving in the depths of water
Pharaoh's half-reflected daughter
Lazing on the strand as on a bed
King David's star a crown upon her head

I waded out into the surf
In search of what I hadn't craved on Earth
Filling my lungs with Ocean as with smoke
Exhaling psalms, which smilingly she answered
Tracing with her fingertips the pattern
Of energy descending into matter
Here on my skin, and laid upon my tongue
Words in which Christ's lullabies were sung

And the waves which clothed her like a foreign name
Parted that my hymns might reach her
Memory broke like morning, and my dreams
Were saturated with her sudden laughter
So much of that eloquence escapes me
As the gradual shift of sense deludes me
I forget what wisdom was mine
But play upon this broken mandolin

Trying

They came at dusk to the distribution tent
For a sleeping bag and a torch, and off they went
Towards an uncertain channel, and an idling truck
We grinned and winked at them, and wished them luck:

Baktiki bash, brakam, I swear I'll see you there
On the other side of this night, when we both are
Middling Englishmen with our English pain
But don't let me see you in this camp again

They would return just before the dawn
With freezing feet and all their clothing torn
People called it "trying": it tried us all
Kept us awake until the frost fell

Over a drunken camp, too cold to sleep
We tried our best but, oh, that chill sank deep

Song from a Crisis

My love washes herself in the sea
That same sea sunken with Syrian dead
Smells of salt and oil and feels
Like a peach on my lips

And the only cruelty in her is distance
Nautical miles of rust-red wine
This hard and haunted ocean filled with you
And human flesh and hunger

I will go down to its margins
Lend my slender shape to the waves
Declaim with the seabirds my poems
For the sake of those yet alive

And crown you with shells from my pocket
Anoint you with lager and sweat
And seek in you the sweetness of living
Lest we forget

Magdalen

Magdalen, before I knew
My Hebrew name I came to you
It was before the call to prayer
Before the desert drank the dew
When you washed me with your hair

I had come to learn the Law
What else was a disciple for?
You slipped into my trembling hand
Like truth into a metaphor
And guided me across the sand

Afterwards, though you went out
Into the dark, you turned about
Coming into the candle light
Where I lay motionless, laid out
Like a victim of the night

You sat and sang the song of songs
Like one to whom the song belongs
Did you sing for Solomon
Or for all the speechless tongues
That nonetheless have tasted dawn?

Night was black and comely then
No night like that has come again
Not here in Gethsemane
But, perhaps, the sea is soft
For other men, in Galilee

Divine Love
Human Love

I slept beside you, did I dream?
But of the nameless and its name
Magdalen, you spoke the word
Into my sleep, and I became
The hearer, hearing, and the heard

When we woke, you took me up
Toward the temple, step by step
Before its gates we listened to
The songs of the ancient faithful slip
From ancient, faithful lips to you

Seven sins they say I cast
Out of your breast, but what came first
Salvation's need or its release?
You were kind, you quenched my thirst
For this I pray you go in peace

Magdalen, before I knew
There was a way I came to you
Then for a while you were the way
As one Jew to another Jew
I guess you taught me how to pray

And I am always in that place
Inside that breach of time and space
But where are you tonight, my love?
Look not to the empty cross
Nor tarry by the hollow grave

Magician's Lovesong

Alone at last, this tortured world
Is banished by the shapes we've curled
Around ourselves: the sacred smoke
The cards we drew, the words we spoke
Our past lies buried in the ground
Horse and rider, both are drowned
And what remains is yours and mine
This midnight rich with blood and wine

I bless your body with my sweat
If you my frailty forget
I rise, a lotus of the Nile
To suck on starlight for a while
I name you prophetess and sister
Better names you'll find at rest here
Sweeter, simpler inspiration
And the nectars of salvation

Viscous on my fingertips
Go through the parting of your lips
As the wind chime rings to heaven
And the Exe sings to the Severn
Bow, but only to yourself
I kneel before you, Lord of life
How strange a shape you choose to take
Two flowers that lean towards a lake

A Prince and Princess of excess
And daring in their faithfulness

They made a world in which to meet
Which sorrow seeds to make it sweet
The stamen and the stigma bow
To meet a bee between the two
The mouth between the yang and yin
Invites the insect body in

So brief delusion of the loss
Dies like a hero on a cross
How brutal then the vital breath
And what a dance we've made of death
(And what a dance we've made of death)
But what a death the dawn will prove
The bruise of smoke inside the mouth
The brittle wounds of living love

In Exeter Cemetery

There is a tall pillar rising up from the grass
And a hundred and sixty names stand out upon it
I will take up this screw and scratch upon it ours
In case nobody ever reads this sonnet

I will immortalise you with the dead
And you will be like them but alive instead
And this book of verse will graffiti you in time
Like a soft-bodied creature flattened by a planet

The Fibonacci curl of something once alive
More elegant even than Shakespeare's rhyme
Or a random selection of bones which survive
Being yet more eloquent than a given name

They are dead and we somehow are not
My love, why then should we not take heart?

Winter Sun

Through soaking pines
Past clusters of coloured tents
The sunlight wanders weakly

Muscles made by mountains
Sink through mud
As the nomad staggers forward

In the kitchen tent
He seeks strong tea and sprawls
Amongst defeated soldiers

Then dances in circles
Bounded by the sea
Until he crosses over those waters

Queen of Night

But who are you to tread so close to me
beneath the boughs of the golden-apple tree?
I was born where seed is never sown
broke a wild mare ere I was grown
rode over raw steppe under a storm
that pricked me on to seek this laurelled throne
quicksilvered by exposure to the stars
This throne cannot be won by strength in wars
nor is it bequeathed to sons of men
unless they bend to die and rise again
This then I would, and bow before your hand
and walk with you throughout the wooded land
Then burn for me, and from the pyre I'll bring
sufficient light to give the night a King

The Money Spider

The money spider
Standing erect on my fingertip
Glowed in the sun
I could see through its body

Then a trail shot out
From my finger onto the wind
And the spider disappeared
Blissfully into the unknown

Trudge

My feet trudge
Through thick mud
Where the earth
Meets the sea
Where the east
Meets the west
Where the Kurds
Rest

The sky flashes
In sewage
Golden fire
Glints in waste waters
The sun sets
Over the jungle
And for a moment
All is still

Drums beat
Cooking fires hiss
Innumerable grubby hands
Rub themselves together
Voices ululate
Green eyes glint
Sparks scatter
Night falls

Besh picks up his guitar
And sings
The Kurdish men
Are dancing in circles
Arms hooked around
One another's shoulders
Black boots stamping down
On cold, wooden slats

Kurdistan in My Mind

I didn't know then, but how could I have,
young, and sick, and blinded by your love,
what that place would mean to me, and how
I'd wish I'd carried on into the snow—
covered Taurus mountains, there to find
some bandit country battered by the wind
savage enough to keep the Turks at bay
and give the Ahl-i-Haqq a place to pray
that I might wander, severed from myself
and from all the despairs of modern life
or fight for Kurdistan somehow and win
approval from the ghosts of Mem and Zin
or even fall, unseen, from some high pass
escaping the gaze of the world, and my disgrace

You Do Have Mercy

You do have mercy on me in your way
though you do not move to comfort me
you sit and hold the silence as we pray
to the God of laughter, love, and liberty

who mocks at our meandering astray
but sitting here, just let His silence be
it fills us with His presence for today
and swells our riverbanks of memory

from desert springs above the dusty towns
brim with water dark as tanks of ink
we flood our mouths in which Atlantis drowns
again, again our sunstruck bodies sink

in that subconscious vacuum which belongs
to you and I so long as we don't think
the thinking one is the one that thinking owns
I'm drowning in these words, come let us drink

It is all tangled up, this mess of you and I
clouds that meet and merge and burst in a burning sky

Roomy Acres

We count exhaustively as we breathe in
The one and hundred names that keep us calm
The gesture is complete, so we begin
Exhaling blissfully this sweet Salaam

It's lost into the city of the night
A muezzin's cry that he must sing again
Until at last you hear him get it right
Diffusing light upon the homes of men

Not to wonder how it should be done
Not as he cries out with a single voice
That there is one alone and only one
For lovers to remember and rejoice

The one and other, faces of a coin
Spin so fast you think they might rejoin

Words Are Birds

I do not fear my dreams should go
I always focus on my breath
there is no way I could get lost
I shun no thought of death
I live inside the living flesh
within the gasp upon the tongue
ever-fleeting, ever fresh
I am the one, eternal song
unless I am the one who sings
empty words on silver wings

Flag

You see that flag?
It must be taken down
This is France
We fly the French flag here
Climb up that tree at once
And take it down

I can't climb that high

Well someone can
Someone put it up there
Find him for us now
Tell us, who put it there
The machine guns ask

I don't know who put it there

What flag is it?

The Kurdish flag

Who here is a Kurd?

Three-thousand of us

One of you must get it down
At once

A child was found
Who scaled the mighty pine
And lowered the flag

Give it here

The machineguns stamp the colours into the dirt
That frightened ISIS
That defied Saddam
The twenty one rays of the sacred sun
Sink under human shit in French Flanders

And one other thing
Learn to speak the language

Baptism

I threw myself down and kissed the sea
Where she lapped at the sandaled feet of the shore
I knew at last what it was to die
And fear death no more

I cast them off, my principles,
Willingly, like Samson's hair
And stood before her by her own light
Shorn and bare

I touched her where the ocean's face
Gave way to my hands and held her to me
She covered me with her indulgent waves
And I drowned in the sea

Lover

I remember the curve of her back
When she knelt as if in prayer
The roundness of her limbs
And the blackness of her hair

Later on she ate an apricot
And vanished in its taste
I saw how lovers must be like
To those who have no lust

Someone Else Lost upon a Pole

I walked through the desert alone and tired,
My head downturned, as my shadow strode beside,
Enormous and gaunt; I felt satisfied
To cover so much country with my feet;

I settled by an oasis, wet my lips,
And felt the feelings flow which had been dry,
How many cities, how much human grief?
As if the woods required our tears for life,

It gave me fodder for my poems, but then
I only sing them under desert stars
To swallowed-up strangers, wandering like clouds
From one immortal Africa to the next,

Planting gardens along the way, regardless
Of who will find his final rest therein

Shekhinah

I am not by that grave but in the city
Solomon built to clothe mount Sion's body
You are everywhere but in me
I alone of you am empty

Ancient sons and daughters wear the looks
Of traders in the wide, absurd bazaar
Mem and Zin in drag meet and are sundered
Salem of her tabernacles plundered

Wanders, naked, through every hashish dream
The Djinn could wish upon our dying scene
And I am like a dove, released
With slipknot cord upon her slender leg

Waiting for you, catastrophe, to appear
And cut me loose or reel me gently in

PART III
Twenty-first Century Karma

Camels

Time comes over the mountains
Carrying the seeds of seasons in his sack
Light slumbers under a fragile quilt
Breaks into a thousand colours as she wakes
The world is an imagination
A ripple on the surface of a lake
Words fall like drops from melting glaciers
Days pass like strangers

I wait for grace, wishing my back were straight
Breaths even out, lungs fill
Like camels at a watering hole

A Rapt Spring

Spring came in with a whisper
A liberator's cry, a consent
Bayonets and barricades sank
Washed out to sea by the river

A word of love, like a rhythm
Played steadily on a guitar
Gave us confidence in time
To waste in perfecting the song

Your voice comes clearly
To me and breezes from night
Until dawn upon my skin
Contain the scent of thaw

Not yet roses, but let them bloom
And they, the children of peace,
Will decorate our afternoons
And we will not be lonely when old

Gypsy, when you sing
I hear what these dreams really are
Churchbells from before churches
Light before dawn

Will you come down to me
From your memory?
I will polish your altar
Where this candle burns

Starets

Dance like Rasputin to the twin guitars
He is mad as us for Bohemia's battle songs
Laugh like one who lives between the wars
And knows how much to peace her rage belongs

This is good, this is your slender neck
Caressed like a silver spoon between my fingers
Like a penny warped, rubbed bright for greatest luck
Blood rushes back but the indentation lingers

This is good, this is your mass of hair
A bed of reeds caught by the fading sun
In one of those real summers, not like this one
But that which flesh conceals until it's born

This is good, this is what the tongue
Tastes when it can taste us both combined
Two broken thoughts unite to form a song
Two hemispheres complete to make the mind

So do not forget this kiss: it marks us out as holy
The Spirit is with us in case we should get lonely
The third thing is movement between the two
Thus trinity is made of me and you

Immolation

He strode from tent to tent
A solitary arsonist
Piled up cans of gas
And lit a match

The jungle immolated
As we dragged the stragglers away
And all was sodden ashes
By dawn next day

A solitary arsonist
Strode from tent to tent
The volunteers cheered
Burn the kitchen next

Burn it all
The shacks and the shelters
Where we warmed our hands
For we worship fire

I Wanted to Tell You

I wanted to tell you
I'm in France
At night the stars move
And my feet are cold

I thought I saw dead soldiers in the woods
Crowding round silently
To watch it carry on

There is warmth at the heart of this
Embers around which roots and fingers are twisted
It beats and we continue

Acting out the past
I wanted to tell you
Aching for them feels good
And it makes me so ashamed

Pursuit

You, I pursue
In my own weak form
Turning back from the white overhang
At the end of the land
I put aside sudden death
Leaving it in my notebooks
With my sketches of the stars
And return into mulch
But the ocean nips my ankles

I watch as your hips switch
Through green meadows
As swallows swoop
Damosel consuming
How long must I follow you
Through miles of English dreams
Before my boots hit dry dirt
And I find myself
At last in Kurdistan?

We travel
Following straight lines
Of telephone poles
Through ashen leagues
Of nomad camps
Spill tea from plastic cups
Over filthy fingers
And lie under stars
But do not dream

The darkness opens
Unpredictably
Like a border
And you gather us up
Dividing our grey faces
Into tribes
And, dressing us in suits
You put us into schools
And have us study poetry

I sigh, and stretch
I crack like an oak in a storm
This page on which
You have your lovers prove
The depths of loss
Cannot contain me
I am a drop in a stream
Staring up at you
From your espresso cup

These seeds of beauty
We have scattered them wide
And watered the furrows
With excess spit
You, alone
Will see them bearing fruit
And smile
Out of your infinite strangeness
Like a cat, purring

A Dangerous Thought

It's funny when you think about it now
The way they say that music is a sin
As if it's something God will not allow
Because nobody does it right but Him

But what's more human than the kicking drum
Slamming in the ever present void?
And mouths which let the breathing body hum
With answered prayers are ever satisfied

You know you hear Him flirt five times a day
In a frenzied preachers' howl at the abyss
With aspirations of the lungs to say
What lips can but conceive of in a kiss

As if He gives us voices just to sing
Immortal songs of human suffering

Cappadocia

In Istanbul
She took me to her favourite place
A cemetery by a row of painted houses
Where we lay down
And she had me tell a story to the dead

We climbed up a hill like a broken tooth
To a city that the lonely Romans built
And sat above the yawning desert
Like two yogis on a Himalaya

She closed her eyes so I closed my eyes
Legs folded underneath us
The sound rolled like a bowling ball
From Horizon to Horizon

Passing through me
Taking a moment to tickle my heart
Like a conscientious lover from within

I am that I am that I am that I am that I am

She rolled like an ocean in my arms
Her eyes were transparent
Mirrors
It seemed like some kind of salvation
But that was the last time we made love

Up upon a height she stood
Like Christ about to be tempted
A chasm opening before her
Like a love-addicted mouth
Spews many coloured balloons
Out of the silence of the desert
And the rose-blossoms of their burners
Light her cheeks on the edge of the world

This really happened
I saw it

Valentine's Sonnet

Why should I cling to my pain?
Even though sadness suited me once, it no longer fits,
My body is big, swollen with the World
My shoulders carry a head sick with dreams,

They will overflow, they were not
Intended to gestate beyond the spring
But must burst out and seek to consummate
This contract which I signed in faery land

That drove me mad, and spiked my songs
Set straight on course for witnessing the end
Of all things, through eyes scrubbed by tears
A body scourged by sickness 'til it was strong

We are so young we have resisted death
In all its attempts to make us take it seriously

Slow Maturing Bliss

Why should I weep, who never had to lose
this World, but was the Earth by touching her?
I tasted all her sweetness and I smiled
to see she loved me too, and how it thrilled

to be consumed by soul, by sense, by self
became the teeth that gnawed the heart of life
and moaned, and died, and Death within me died
and in his place was new born deathless light

whose white contained innumerable shades
of colour, the black void giving birth to stars
so I drowned in that abyss, and scattered seeds
that sucked your spring, burst blossom in the dark
and everything is love, and always was
thank you for reminding me of that

Happy

I wanted to be happy and I was
Underneath the unobscured stars
I wanted to be happy and I was
Hidden by cars and hipster bars

I wanted to be happy and I was
Lost among squat punks in France
I wanted to be happy and I was
Confusing the dancers for the dance

I wanted to be happy and I was
In terminals and camps through which nomads move
I wanted to be happy and I was
High on some ghostly mountain, in love

I wanted to be happy and I was
On European streets gloomy with age
I wanted to be happy and I was
Washing my boots in your Atlantic rage

I wanted to be happy and I was
On the edge of all things, tasting dawn
And drinking night, and thanking love
For all it has endowed me with

I wanted to be happy and I was
With everything that tore me through the flesh

The unrepented injury that forms
The heart of action, strength inside a crush
I wanted to be happy and I was
With the dew-stricken morning, the hurricane, the calm
I wanted to be happy, and I am

Magda Lynn

Magda Lynn
I am going home
Going back
To where I'm from
Far away
From what I knew
When I was one
With you

Here I am
But weak and sick
And the sand
So cold and thick
Gets into
Your dreams you see
I guess you dreamed
Of me

Otherwise
Why would I stand
Like a cross
In desert land?
On a hill
I looked for you
And found you
Looking
Too

History
so hard to read
A litany of doubt and greed
But you were sure and you were soft
And held my ragged wings aloft

Magda Lynn
I am going home
Going back
To where I'm from
Far away
From what I knew
When I was one
With you

Edible Bugs

Seagulls tap the turf, enticing worms
To sudden death, the weak must feed the strong
And strength abandon subtle ways to find
Complete defeat though it becomes itself
It must bow, bend to the brink, and shatter
Brittle from the white heat of perception

Becoming an eye to love will make one blind,
Over-brimmed with mercy, love struck stoned,
A drunkard tapping his foot to your constant beat
As you disarm him of his cruelty, pickpocket

Your fingers are in all my conspiracies
Your gradual changes in the muscles of my wings
Make them always stronger for wounds you put in them
The caterpillar no longer fears your beak

Nick of Time

Are we whole and are we holy
Who in England wait to die
Though the years roll on slowly
Like white clouds in a midday sky?

Are we free and are we able
For the arms our fathers bore?
No not we, for we are living
While the dead men go to war

Are we strong and are we true men?
Ask not I, who never stood
To ask my own heart in a moment
When blood's strength was asked of blood

Who was not keen, and was not willing
When youth's fire was still astir
To go between the killing
And the weak, while others were

See Saw

She saw good and ill in me
But I saw only love in her
A memory, a memory
The kind that I prefer

I met her when the hills were green
I said do you know what I mean?
Can anyone? Can anyone
Describe the white of the sun?

She saw good and ill in me
But I saw only love in her
A memory, a memory
The kind that I prefer

She pointed to her lips and said
Here are all the books I've read
A mouth, a tongue, a treasury
I said, teach me your glossary

She saw good and ill in me
But I saw only love in her
A memory, a memory
The kind that I prefer

She led me down to Harewood Close
And dared me to a yoga pose
I stretched and stretched but could not find
The end of secrets in her mind

She saw good and ill in me
But I saw only love in her
A memory, a memory
The kind that I prefer

She said you will not find me here
Not here where I am oh so near
Go far away from Harewood, close
Enough to hear the raw wood's voice

She saw good and ill in me
But I saw only love in her
A memory, a memory
The kind that I prefer

I made a camp in Arcady
Where she could freely come to me
And there in silence sought the words
With which to wing these grey, clay birds

She saw good and ill in me
But I saw only love in her
A memory, a memory
The kind that I prefer

Giraffe

Jane has almost made a giraffe
Out of clay
The muscles are there
Beneath the skin
Only the breath is missing
Moving in and out of his nostrils
I said, I find it's like that with poems
They come as you sculpt them
Out of formless beginnings
The shape of life can emerge
And the more you take away
The more is there
First it's just a lump of clay
Then, a giraffe

Sappho

It is because she lifted that head from the sea
And tasted, though undesiring, its speechless lips
Taking upon her own his silent tongue
Forming its first and final harmony
As from his neck, still-fresh drops
Freckled her face, that she learned to sing

Ships were seeds scattered on the sunlit main
But music grew in her like the young night
As the ears of stars pricked up from furrowed cloud
Therefore she looked out not for the fleet's return
Though she stood intoning epigrams to the tide
But for the face that rippled in the flood

Stillness mirrored, ever moving, she
Spoke, and the Ocean wrote her poetry

Meteor

I crashed like a meteor back into England
And threw out dank smoke from a crater
Nothing was low enough, nothing tasted
Sufficiently of authentic despair

Except the cold concrete beneath my boots
Stomping, hungover down to the quay
Looking for coffee as though it were a fight
Looking for the sea to rise up

Consume the estuary and drown me last
Bobbing, as I would, amidst baby Kurds
The ruins of Atlantis, and coelacanths
I would there become sufficiently nothing

A particle in a greater whole
A hole inside the whole

Wavicle

If all you ever have is ideas
What chance is yours of touching real life?
They would be purest fantasy and safe
Were they not gripped at one end by the foe
Who'll use whatever it is you seem to love
To weaponise your longing and make real
The grimmest nightmare as you drown in dreams

I would not worship a God I had not touched
Who had not touched me, true materialist
I demanded that he show his wounds to me
And tugged his beard in case it was a fake
And said: Okay, if you are the Messiah
Save my soul for me, in spite of me
And I looked and saw my own side bleeding

Saviour Poem

But really if it wasn't for the cross
His body wouldn't fit upon that chain
As it is he decorates your skin
Subtle fingers toy with wayward locks
The dark, enduring waters of your hair
Tortured and oppressed you took him in
Hardly noticing the worldly looks
For his thorns conspired to make him thin
Like you'd found him in some holy book
Fleeing like a dream of innocence
Down the shining streets of Exeter
Ragged as a real eternal Jew
I don't suppose you would have stayed except
For all the prayers he stuttered out to you

I Can't Believe It's Not Buddha

Whatever you fight for fights for you
Whatever you fight against resists
You spin upon a crazy wheel
Not knowing you know but feeling you feel
Not knowing the cause but thinking it real
And all the while the pain persists

You make a story out of time
Time makes a story out of you
Chasing after what you were
Or holiness and its allure
Detesting what is false for sure
For sake of loving what is true

You try to cross the stream again
But gentle waters block your way
You try to make yourself like stone
Or anything that stands alone
But what you stood upon is gone
And what you were has washed away

You cannot live, you will not die
You pay for breath with bitter sweat
It seems like every joke's on you
But did you ever wonder who
Set you sifting false from true
Or what made you forget?

You grasp it then it slips again
As though it's made for teasing you
It haunts you in the giggling ring
Of chimes that rhyme and bells that sing
It's meaningless like everything
You made for sake of pleasing you

Mantra

I am not the thoughts but the one
Perceiving the thoughts I am not the thoughts
But the one perceiving the thoughts I am not
The thoughts but the one perceiving the thoughts

I am not the thoughts but the one
Perceiving the thoughts I am not the thoughts
But the one perceiving the thoughts I am not
The thoughts but the one perceiving the thoughts

I am not the thoughts but the one
Perceiving the thoughts I am not the thoughts
But the one perceiving the thoughts I am not
The thoughts but the one perceiving the thoughts

I am not the thoughts but the one
Perceiving the thoughts I am not

Evacuation

When I was a boy, I heard the tale
Of soldiers stranded on a beach
How little boats plucked them all
From death's reach

And what a picture to hold in the eye
Tiny ships with their white sails
Ploughing on through cannon fire
On the road of whales

In latter days other weary troops
Puffed on frozen fingers by the surging sea
And waited for Britain to open her gates
To the Peshmerga and the YPG

Fresh from war with England's foes
Breaking bomb blasts aimed for us
Dying for a dream we have overthrown
Never guessing at our spinelessness

I have always believed that England is good
Politics haven't shaken that
From left or right, it's understood
She shoots with a straight bat

So when I found those broken soldiers
Stranded in the Gallic mud
I scanned the horizons for crusaders
Coming on a flood

To carry the defenders of our land
Far from the bloody field of shame
I admit I cannot understand
Why no-one came

No-one came and there was no
Relief but in the thought of spring
As the winter sapped us of our hope
And we sagged in the sea on our sodden wings

Seabirds blown from the shores we knew
Each one of us a refugee
Keeping watch with the lucky few
Who still had hope in the sundering sea

Alchemist

Buzzards call to us from tombstone peaks
that shadow over our starry grave
they speak of life and death that life remakes
of fulsome earth and of heaven's void above
yes we will break, but as the day breaks
and die like light so, come the dawn, we live

Alchemist you are waters in the dark
in which I've plunged to hunt my sunken name
have I not always spied you from this bark?
So sea-bird-like we play a fishing game
shaking off the water now, forsake
the one thing left that Heaven could think to blame

Truly now there's nothing that I know
and knowing naught have nowhere left to go
If I could breathe your body in and through
my mind I'd make your mind my body too
I cannot stop myself from striving to
distil this dawn to pour its light on you

Desert Father

I am the eternal soul of man,
shorn of race, and rank, and even name,
awash amidst the climaxes of fate,
mariner on a frothing sea of time,
I was in Rome when Augustus was made a God,
I touched the trees that fell so Venice stands,
I walked upon the frozen face of Thames,
remembering then the nakedness of Nile
when she too froze, and Egypt free of sand,
the Sphinx was young, the language fresh with power
for primal poetry, wafting like smoke
of frankincense or dankly sweet hashish,
my mind was young and keen for desert songs,
I dressed myself in you and dreamed of this

Adam and Eve It

The world is wearing words out of need
To shout itself awake in you at last
This voice is born of nothing that is dead
It makes the future, echoes not the past

Is what you wanted gone and what you have
Sufficient to build what will be always yours?
Good, then let's continue to believe
In creativity, it breathes, it pours

Out of the chalice which will always renew
The pattern though it cares not how it goes
Or why it chooses to be one with you
Who watch the river run and know its flows

Are what are pouring underneath your eyes
In turns of tears dissolving this disguise

Knowledge Is Porridge

I ruled Russia, I stormed against the sea
In a dream, I built my city on a mountain,
I undermined, the capitals were my sequins,
I wove flesh into a coat and wore it,

I sank into the night, you do not know
The pleasure of being tickled by stars,
I was nothing, death would think me nothing,
No target, no threat, no mass, no weight, nothing,

My thoughts passed like light between galaxies,
My breath was the life of worlds although I was dead,
I was a dream, dreaming of itself,
An emptiness that gave birth to itself,
And created, life from a first green seed,
Sap and spit and blood and all the rest of it

NOTES†

PART I: Songs About Nothing

Fall This reflects on the loss of the primordial "poetry of life" and the resulting state between (in Platonic terms) the *exitus* and *reditus*, described as being between the breathing out and breathing in of God.

Memorial The poet writes from his experience of helping refugees in this camp. The young man died in an attempt to find refuge in England, crossing there under a truck.

Landing Where we have landed from the Fall the Creator Spirit appears to be absent, now only a memory of "a hot, faint, shimmer of breath." Nonetheless, the quest for love awakens in human flesh.

Fog of War This refers to the gassing of the Kurds in Saddam Hussein's Iraq.

Nameless Nothing The title alludes to the ineffable, the Divine, which is "nothing in particular" in Abbot John Chapman's words. The word ("lips") of God replaces what was communicated in the touch of creation, as imaged in Michelangelo's picture. This latter primordial bond is now mediated by symbolic gesture ("mudra") and remembered obscurely.

† The reader is strongly encouraged to explore the poems in depth for him or herself before having recourse to the notes. These do not intend to offer a definitive reading: only to suggest one possible way into the poems. Spending time with the poems without them will give the reader ways in of his or her own.

Elevation The Yezidis are Kurds who were besieged on Mount Sinjar by Daesh in August 2014. The People's Units are the YPG, a Kurdish defence force.

Grail Fish The "nameless nothing" of the earlier poem is present in varied ways: in the burning bush from which the voice said to Moses, "I AM THAT I AM," in the Irish hero Finnegan's catching of the Salmon of knowledge and in other manifestations of the Spirit and of love.

Gender Roles The women are the YPJ, the women's branch of the Kurdish defence force, the People's Protection Units.

Voice in Wilderness The title alludes to Saint John the Baptist (Mark 1.2). The "wind" suggests the Spirit and the "old tent" the covering given by words. The "woman" points to the mother of the Light of the World, which "appears in rays."

Economics The poet is referring to the refugees he got to know in the refugee camp in Dunkirk.

The Invention of Fire Fire is a symbol of the Spirit, as at Pentecost (Acts 2.3) and at the celebration of the Easter Vigil, and so are "dawn" and "light." As "we slip into sound" there is articulation of "the name of nothing." Yet "No thing is left"—in one sense we are bereft, even of that "nameless nothing" that lingered as a memory of the source, "the primal spark"; in another the presence of the Divine is no longer "secret" and apparently "nothing"—it is "found" and "not even doubts remain." It is from beyond this world and indeed comes from "No thing."

Magdalene Saint Mary Magdalene witnesses to the Resurrection, having seen the empty tomb (Matthew 28.1–8): this is the "volcanic cave" into which its light pours. She has learnt love from the Master. It is being "alone," that is: one, not separated.

Absent The absence of the title and the refrain is the "nameless nothing" of the poem above, the divine presence which cannot be there as "something" because it transcends every created thing. No adornment can replace it. The phrase also articulates the divine discontent, the longing for the perfect love of God: to love someone (and this is a love-song) is to want God, because only God can fulfil the project. The riches of the world, the poet reflects, "cannot decorate my love."

Jeremiad Jeremiah was a prophet who warned of divine wrath on account of the corruption of society. The atom bomb symbolises the spiritual peril our society faces.

Drag The poet wants to number himself among God's chosen people who crossed the Red Sea, traditionally a figure of crossing from this world into eternity.

Jerk Hypnic A hypnic jerk is when you experience a sense of falling and landing just as you are about to fall asleep. The reversal of the phrase is a clue suggesting that the poem be read backwards. Either way, it presents love, the source of creation, overcoming divisions. They are simply love's manifestation and love brings us to rest in peace.

Sun of Man The title alludes to the One who is both the goal of humanity (sun) and humanity as such (Son of Man). He, "infinity in flesh," lives in each beachcomber on the shore of eternity, each person here "for love." Out of love, He "took the name of shame," and in defeat finds victory and the eternal life of Divine Unity.

Agamemnon This is a poem about power lust.

Doe This is both a direct personal observation of nature and a poetic capture of how the primordial oneness of creation is lost:

the move to duality is between the eighth and the ninth lines of the sonnet. The "dirty human hands" evoke the story of the fall.

Blank Page "Bury with their words" recalls Saint Paul: "the letter killeth but the spirit giveth life" (2 Corinthians 3.6). "Suras" are chapters of the Koran. The poet seeks to communicate divine truth. He reflects on how thought is shared through writing and wonders what will happen if he gets it wrong.

Anatolia Anatolia, which means "east" or "sunrise," is the most western part of Asia, comprising most of what is now called Turkey. The Aegean Sea divides Asia and Europe. Kurdistan images the Promised Land for the poet—see, for example, *Kurdistan in My Mind* below.

The Transmigration of Souls "*Non interire*" is "not to die" or "not to be extinguished" and is the first half of a catechism representing the ancient Celtic doctrine of reincarnation: "*non interire sed transire.*" The refrain "I die and am reborn" also evokes the spiritual rebirth associated with Christian baptism, an entrance into the life "beyond / Both dusk and dawn"—eternal life. "This migrant song" is sung in a refugee camp.

Objects in Space "*sed transire*"—see note on previous poem. Refugees, who have nowhere to settle, are considered to be as alien as objects in outer space until the truth is inescapable that they share our flesh and blood.

Falling Leaves "God is light" (1 John 1.5) and like the light in this poem cannot be held and made use of. In His light all things are passing, like autumn leaves, and superseded by new life. The love expressed in the final two lines makes sense of immersion in this process.

Sister Exe The Exe is the river that runs through Exeter, a city in the west of England. Her personification recalls Saint Francis's "Sister Water." Water, in its yielding omnipresence, is a symbol of the Spirit of God "which moved on the face on the waters" (Genesis 1.2) at the creation. That Spirit is fire also and reaches us through "the power of the Highest" (Luke 1.35) overshadowing the immaculately loving Woman. The poet wonders if his reaching out to Her with love is as futile as the attempt of Orpheus to bring back Eurydice from the dead. Can his words bring Her to the light? Is his poetry illusion or the form in which the formless—the "nameless nothing"—is joyously, laughingly present? The "many names" of love are more ancient than our attempts to take possession of Her through expression as though the cycle of time represented by the ouroborus, the serpent biting its tail, and time's redemption through the fruit of the Virgin's womb were our property. As the poem meanders through mythology like the eponymous Exe, some of them are rehearsed and through them the mystery verges on articulation before each new twist in the river. The "sacred feminine" cannot be won. The poet says he does not pray for that, "But that I might sing her hymn, a sinner, / Here on my pin-up altar, O ma donna."

The Absent God This sonnet can be read as referring to creation "ex nihilo" and ontology if we take the first eight lines being spoken by God. "I AM" is the identity He gives Himself (Exodus 3.14), but fundamentally being is only a symbol of Him (like light) so He knows not "what it is to be." He is rather the source of being. He is also love—so He gazes at the poet his "sweet enigma" (enigma because how can anything exist that is not God?) with self-emptying (kenotic) love. His creature is held in being by His gaze ("eye"—also His identity as Self/I), although made out of nothing ("naked void"—no thing). Only in the apophatically apprehended silence of God (God is not a thing) can anything be said of the creature who comes from nothing and in that silence there are volumes (including all that the poet is inspirited to write)—"all about you" because God is in love with His creature. The silence speaks of God also: "Nothing is more like God than silence," said Meister Eckhart. The four lines that follow indicate that though God can say (or simply think) us into being we cannot say Him. The final two lines give the speaking back to God. Our knowledge of God is hidden as He is hidden in us, but is—"already"—there. Yet insofar as it is articulated it is necessarily reductive, understood in terms of creation ("colours") although it does say something cataphatically since, as God is symbolised by being he is also (as Scripture testifies) symbolised by light. So the last word of the poem is an epiphany. Since our knowing and loving is necessarily a reflection of God's knowing and loving, these lines can speak of that as well as of His knowing and loving. This outline can only point to what is happening in the poem, an inspired speaking of the numinous.

Brothers The poet identifies fraternally with the refugees. Oil: a *casus belli* in the Middle East.

PART II: Kurdish Songs

Ishqt "Ishqt" is Arabic for "your love" and also the title of a famous Kurdish pop song which the poet heard sung in the Dunkirk refugee camp.

I Remember Phoenix Phoenix is a fellow volunteer working in the refugee camp. The poet stayed in "the farm at Herzeele," a small village nearby.

A Vault in the Desert The title puns on T.E. Lawrence's *The Revolt in the Desert*. What happens to the bones images the duality that is the concomitant of creation. It alludes to the posthumous fate of Mem and Zin, lovers in an ancient Kurdish story like "Romeo and Juliet." It also speaks of the dead of the First World

War, the separation between modern day nations, and the calamities that separate people in their everyday lives.

Spartans Kurdish warriors, who escaped being massacred by Daesh on Mount Sinjar and are now struggling with life in a refugee camp, are compared to Spartans at war.

Yes Tor "Yes Tor" is a high point on Dartmoor in the west of England. The height of the Tor is a symbol of closeness to God. The view speaks of Kurdistan and the descent of the fall of man. The "other, promised land" suggests the Kurdish aspiration for a homeland, as well as heaven.

Herẓeele See introduction.

Desert Confession Jesus has the feelings of a sinner because God "hath made him to be sin for us" (2 Corinthians 5.21) and "he hath borne our griefs and carried our sorrows" (Isaiah 53.4).

Prodigious Sun The "prodigious sun" is the hot sun, oppressive to one who thirsts, the wonderful Son who redeems, and the prodigal son with whom He redeemingly identifies, allowing him too to become wonderful. "Mother" is the Blessed Virgin Mary. Water is a symbol of the Holy Spirit, sent among us for the forgiveness of sins. The sky is a symbol of heaven. The simplicity of the monosyllables of the final line powerfully expresses the directness of its feeling.

Seasong The song of the sea alludes to the song sung by the Israelites after the crossing of the Red Sea, a figure in Christian tradition of the Easter triumph over sin and of baptism. "Home" is Israel, the Promised Land but also the starting point from which the traveller sets out and to which he returns with what he has learnt. The "draft" is the water but also "draught" as in a vintage wine that inebriates as the infinite (symbolised by sea) inebriates the soul. Mary, Queen of the Sea, sang "Christ's lullabies." As the epiphany of inspiration fades, the poet can convey only something of it, as it were upon "a broken mandolin."

Trying "Baktiki bash, brakam" is Sorani Kurdish for "good luck, my brother."

Song from a Crisis The title refers to the refugee crisis. "The sea": the Aegean Sea where many Syrian refugees have perished trying to cross from Turkey to Greece.

Magdalen Jesus addresses Mary Magdalen. His Hebrew name means "God Saves." It is in relation to "salvation's need" in her that He knows who He is. The "song of songs" is the great love song in the Bible, the Song of Solomon; "black and comely" is an allusion to it (1.5). "The nameless and its name" is the mystery of divine love. "The hearer, the hearing and the heard" is the Holy Trinity, the perfect paradigm of love. The final two lines point to its triumph in the resurrection, and the angel's word to Mary Magdalen, "He is not here: for he is risen, as he said" (Matthew 28.6).

Magician's Lovesong "Horse and rider, both are drowned": a reference to the Red Sea closing over the Egyptians pursuing Moses and the Israelites escaping Egypt or (figuratively) sin. "Yours and mine": the Divine love which transcends private ownership. "Blood and wine" are associated as in George Herbert's lines, "Love is that liquor sweet and most divine, / Which my God feels as blood; but I, as wine." "Prophetess and sister": Miriam (sister of Moses and Aaron) who takes up the song of triumph about the victory over the Egyptians (Exodus 15.21). "They made a world in which to meet / Which sorrow seeds to make it sweet?" echoes Shakespeare's "parting is such sweet sorrow" and alludes to the creation of the world by the separation (duality) of "the waters which were under the firmament from the waters which were above the firmament" (Genesis 1.7). "The brief delusion of the loss" is that duality, represented by "the stamen and the stigma," which is overcome by love. "What a dance we've made of death" alludes to "Love is strong as death" (Song of Solomon 8.6).

In Exeter Cemetery The pillar in the cemetery is a memorial to the 160 people killed when Exeter Theatre burnt down in the mid-1800s. "Shakespeare's rhyme" is particularly that of his sonnets which offered immortality to his love, as in, for example, "But were some child of yours alive that time, / You should live twice, in it and in my rhyme" and "You still shall live (such virtue hath my pen) / Where breath most breathes, even in the mouths of men."

Winter Sun This is set in the refugee camp. The sun features on the Kurdish flag and is the spirit of the refugees, dancing and unconfined in adversity, though they are physically constrained.

Queen of Night This poem gives dramatic form to the meeting of the Aryan warrior culture with the Mediterranean and African goddess culture (see *The White Goddess* by Robert Graves). It echoes the universal spiritual truth expressed thus in the Bible: "Verily, verily, I say unto you, Except a corn of wheat fall into the ground and die, it abideth alone: but if it die, it bringeth forth much fruit" (John 12.24).

The Money Spider This images the dissolving of the egotistic self and the entry of soul into bliss.

Trudge The rhythm of the poem expresses the title onomatopoei-cally. The setting is the refugee camp near Dunkirk, known as "the jungle." Besh is a Kurdish refugee.

Kurdistan in My Mind Ahl-i-Haqq: followers of the religion of Yarsanism, who are persecuted. Mem and Zin are the star-crossed lovers in an ancient Kurdish story, whose union is thought to represent the return of the Kurds to their homeland.

127

You Do Have Mercy Praying, the poet knows the presence of God in the silence. In that remembrance he is one with the other, freed from capture by thought.

Roomy Acres The title puns on the name of Rumi (a thirteenth-century Persian Sufi mystical poet) with his invocation of the multiple names of God—each of the latter being a distinct identity (acre / AKA: "also known as")—and the spaciousness of what he apprehends in his prayer and verse. The poem reflects on the achievement of the proclamation of unity. The syntactical link between the line "For lovers to remember and rejoice" with what goes before it ("one alone and only one") and with what comes after it ("the one and other") creates an ambiguity that reflects the movement between the experience of unity and that of separation. The image of the final couplet expresses a sense of transcending the division between one and other.

Words Are Birds The assonance in the title is part of the meaning: the vowel of "words" and "birds" is the same in sound. This indicates that spiritually (the vowel corresponds to breath) they are identified. The poet focuses on his breath (that is, the Spirit) and so finds his way. "I live inside the living flesh": as in "The Word was made flesh" and "Because I live, ye shall live also" (John 1.14 & 14.19). "The one who sings" suggests the Father generating the Son ("the eternal song") through the Spirit ("silver wings"). The singer and the song are identified: "he that hath seen me hath seen the Father" (John 14.9). They speak in and through the poet: "we will come unto to him and make our abode with him" (John 14.23). He adds, "Unless I am the one who sings / empty words on silver wings," meaning if he is not being untruthful but also if he is not taking an apophatic approach and simply being open to the unutterable mystery. The poem is characteristic of the poet and his ability to make words, like birds, fly heavenwards.

Flag The authorities asked for the Kurdish flag, which features the sun with its rays, to be taken down when it was flown in the refugee camp near Dunkirk.

Baptism Cf "Know ye not, that so many of us as were baptized into Christ Jesus were baptized into his death?" (Romans 6.3) "My principles" suggests self-will and "I" in the last line egoism "drowned in the sea" as the Egyptians in the Red Sea.

Lover The final two lines are ambiguous: they say that "lovers must be like . . . those who have no lust"—love without seeking selfish gratification; but also the poet sees how lovers appear "To those who have no lust"—the self of the one who loves, in this lust-free perspective, simply disappears in the act of apprehension, hence, ". . . she ate an apricot / And vanished in its taste."

Someone Else Lost upon a Pole Simon Stylites lived on a pillar to be separated from the world. The poet identifies with him, finding retreat in the desert which in monastic tradition is the place of encounter with God. The sadness of the cities gives him narrative material to be shared "under desert stars," that is, in a spiritual context with those in quest of the eternally new (*semper aliquid novi Africam adferre*). He plants "gardens," that is, sows the seeds of paradise, without attachment to the results of his labours.

Shekhinah "Shekhinah" is the divine presence in its feminine aspect. The first line refers to the empty tomb of the Lord. The second couplet of the first stanza alludes to the mystery of there being anyone apart from God. The first couplet of the second stanza indicates that ancient wisdom is as it were put up for sale. "Salem" meaning peace (as in "Jerusalem") no longer has a home. The "dove" is a symbol of the Holy Spirit. "Catastrophe" is the opening through which She can enter.

PART III: Twenty-first Century Karma

Camels The poem is a creation myth.

A Rapt Spring This poem is about the beginning of time and its renewal. "Churchbells from before churches" and "light before dawn" are intimations of the primordial holiness before it was manifested in religion and creation. It is reverenced.

Starets A starets is a wise, holy man in the Russian tradition, such as Rasputin claimed to be. "The twin guitars" represent duality, the dance unity. The human love expressed in the poem embodies this oneness. It is imaged when "Two broken thoughts unite to form a song / Two hemispheres complete to make the mind." It is enacted "in this kiss." It is the Holy Spirit, proceeding from the Father and the Son.

Immolation The poet was present when the Dunkirk refugee camp ("the jungle") was burnt down as described. "We worship fire": fire is sacred to Yazidis, who are Kurds.

I Wanted to Tell You The refugee camp from which the poet speaks is the site where many soldiers fell in the First and Second World Wars. He is aware of them and their heroism.

Pursuit In the poet's pursuit of the sacred, he longs for its instantiation in Kurdistan. It takes him through refugee camps, and he struggles to express in lines of poetry a longing greater than can be written for what is greater than he is. God alone knows what will become of "these seeds of beauty" and be gladdened by them.

A Dangerous Thought The strong rhythm of the first stanza introduces the musical theme. Music is presented as love—"what lips can but conceive of in a kiss"—offered by God and reciprocated by us. We "hum / With answered prayers," using voices He has given us "to sing / Immortal songs of human suffering": music that gives the troubles of our lives eternal meaning.

Cappadocia In his human love, the poet experiences the divine presence, "I am that I am" (Exodus 3.14). The "chasm . . . the silence of the desert" and "the edge of the world" indicate its vastness. Its power to draw up to heaven is imaged by the hot-air "balloons" with their "burners," often seen in Cappadocia.

Valentine's Sonnet "This contract that I signed in faery land" is the poet's commitment to express the poetic inspiration he receives. "The end / Of all things" is the apocalypse, imaged particularly in the fire that destroyed the refugee camp where the poet worked. It is also the world as it is in these last times. "A body scourged by sickness 'til it was strong" refers to the purifying effect of troubles and also evokes Saint Paul's paradoxical insight, "When I am weak, then am I strong" (2 Corinthians 12.10). "We have resisted death..." is an allusion to "Love is strong as death" (Song of Solomon 8.6).

Slow Maturing Bliss See introduction.

Happy This traces the movement in ("hipster bars") and out ("among squat punks") of society to an ultimate grateful ("thanking love") and contented acceptance of everything.

Magda Lynn The title alludes to Vera Lynn, the popular singer and "the Forces' Sweetheart" during World War Two, but is also Saint Mary Magdalene who is spoken to by the Saviour, fighting evil on the "hill" of Calvary.

Edible Bugs See introduction.

Nick of time The heroism of those who have gone before challenges us.

See Saw The title, punning on the first two words of the refrain, alludes to the oscillation between her view and his. She is his inspiration, enabling him to express what he means by giving him her "glossary," meaning both "list of words with explanations" and "tongue." In the simplicity of "Arcady" he seeks words from her to bring to life his "clay birds" as in the following poem.

Giraffe "The breath" is the Spirit which gives life to poems. Their "formless beginnings" emerge from the "Nameless Nothing" (as in the poem of that title) of the ineffable, the divine.

Sappho Sappho is the supreme poet. In the sea, she finds the head of the supreme musician, Orpheus. The sea in this poem is an image of the eternal, the divine. Because this latter, the "Nameless Nothing," is ineffable—and not only because Orpheus is dead—the head has "speechless lips" and "silent tongue." She becomes lips and tongue for the eternal music. She is "stillness mirrored" because she reflects the divine quietude. She therefore has no need to look at "the fleet's return," what becomes of the creation, "seeds scattered on the sunlit main." Her poetry is inspired by the eternal and divine, imaged by the sea.

Meteor The poet returns to England from working with refugees in northern France. The "baby Kurds" are victims of the perilous sea-crossings of refugees. The poet's aspiration to be "sufficiently nothing" corresponds with the teaching of the beatitude, "Blessed are the poor in spirit: for theirs is the kingdom of heaven" (Matthew 5.3). The "greater whole" is that kingdom, entering which being "a hole" (empty of egoism, poor in spirit) makes possible. This latter is the way to holiness—and the "hole" that the meteor makes on impact.

Wavicle Physics teaches that light is both energy and matter; the poet argues that thought without the material is dangerously liable to impose itself on the world murderously. In the person of doubting Thomas he demands incarnation rather than ideology. Thomas is rewarded by being given a share in the wounded Christ's identity.

Saviour Poem The Saviour identifies with the "tortured and oppressed" and is taken in as such. "Eternal Jew" alludes to the archetypal wandering Jew and also to a Nazi propaganda film of that name. "The prayers he stuttered out to you" reverses the expectation that prayers will be addressed to the Saviour and points to His agonised longing for our acceptance of salvation as when He cries "I thirst" upon the cross. His prayer to us to accept the life He offers shows the utter humility and generosity of Christ.

I Can't Believe It's Not Buddha This pitch-perfect evocation of Buddhist spirituality evokes the forgetfulness of one caught in the illusion of this world and the futility of trying to escape from it by self-assertion. It presents the universal truth that only in self-surrender do we transcend the meaningless.

Mantra The repeated mantra leads (in the final couplet) to a moment of enlightenment in which the meditator realises unity: "I am not the thoughts but the one" and in his awareness ("perceiving the thoughts") experiences the dissolution of his ego ("I am not").

Evacuation This refers to the evacuation from Dunkirk in 1940. The Peshmerga are the army of Iraqi Kurdistan.

Alchemist The first stanza speaks of spiritual death and rebirth as imaged in the night and the dawn; the second addresses the alchemist with his powers of transmutation imaged in baptismal waters in which we lose our life to find it; the third is his reply in which he expresses his urge to communicate the essence of this new, selfless life.

Desert Father Man as such speaks through the poet. The title evokes the spiritual wisdom tradition of the monastic elders in the desert. This desert signifies the absence of particular identity enabling a universal identification.

Adam and Eve It The sonnet is about creativity. See introduction.

Knowledge Is Porridge The sonnet is a creation myth. God's knowing something creates it, hence the title. "I ruled Russia": ruling Russia is proverbially impossible, but "with God all things are possible" (Mark 10.27). The monosyllabic directness of the last line contrasts the materiality of the created with the "nothing" of the uncreated.

Lightning Source UK Ltd.
Milton Keynes UK
UKHW01f1028040718

325212UK00001B/19/P